Writing with Power

Second Edition

Michael McHugh

Christian Liberty Academy
Handwriting Program

Written by Michael J. McHugh
Copy editing by Christopher Kou
Cover design by Robert Fine
Layout and graphics by Christopher and Timothy Kou at
imagineering studios, inc.

A publication of
Christian Liberty Press
502 West Euclid Avenue
Arlington Heights, IL 60004
www.christianlibertypress.com

ISBN 978-1-930367-41-8

Text set in Berkeley
Handwriting set in Zaner-Bloser except for "Q" and "k," and ","
Printed in the United States of America

Contents

Lowercase Cursive Alphabet

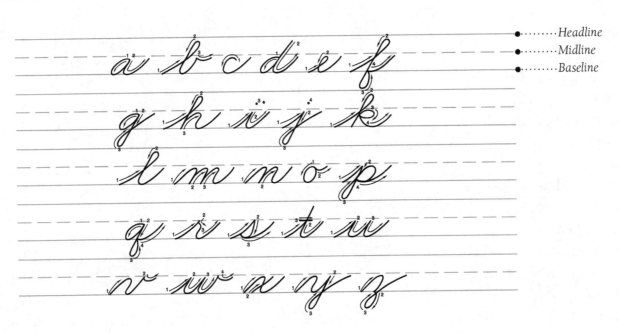

Headline
Midline
Baseline

Uppercase Cursive Alphabet

Headline
Midline
Baseline

Numbers

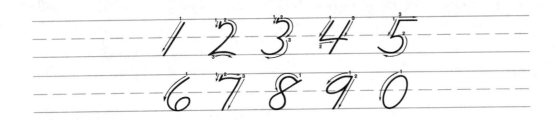

Preface

This is the fifth text in the Christian Liberty Academy handwriting series. We remind you that one key to teaching success is reducing frustration in both parent and student. A wise teacher will not fail to take into account the maturity of the children so they can enjoy their handwriting activities without constant boredom or extreme fatigue. Learning need not be a tedious exercise. The staff at Christian Liberty Academy has taken care to design each lesson to fit the attention span of the average primary student. Patience, prayer, and persistence are indispensable for success in teaching primary handwriting.

It is very important for instructors to realize that extra drill work (on the blackboard and practice paper) must be assigned for each and every concept in the textbook. In addition, have the students practice each exercise before writing their work in the book.

Both gross and fine motor skills are involved in handwriting. Certain abilities are generally found at this level of development:

1. Good control of pencils, scissors, buttons, and zippers.
2. Ability to follow a series of spoken or written directions.
3. Ability to trace lines.
4. Ability to draw figures such as circles and squares.
5. Ability to distinguish between proper and improper spacing.

This text contains activities to develop and maintain the above skills.

Good handwriting is an essential skill of expression and communication. Time spent on handwriting is well spent. May the God of all grace help you develop students who will desire to write legibly and attractively for the glory of God.

In Christian fellowship,
Michael J. McHugh

Proper Writing Posture

Some children write with their left hand. This picture shows how they should sit when they write.

Some children write with their right hand. This picture shows how they should sit when they write.

Some children write with their left hand. This picture shows how they should hold their pencil.

Some children write with their right hand. This picture shows how they should hold their pencil.

Some children write with their left hand. This picture shows how they should stand at the chalkboard.

Some children write with their right hand. This picture shows how they should stand at the chalkboard.

Introduction to Parents

In this text you will be asking your students to take more responsibility for their handwriting skills. This text will cover the principles of advanced cursive. Therefore, you will be asking your students to evaluate their own developing writing ability.

Before you begin, make sure your students have the proper readiness skills:

1. Can the students hold the pencil in a correct fashion?
2. Do the students recognize the difference in forms of letters and words?
3. Do the students appreciate handwriting as a means of communication?
4. Are the students reasonably able to copy a letter?

To improve fine motor skills and eye-coordination, make sure your students have ample opportunity to cut and paste, use paint brushes, draw with chalk on a board, create with clay, play ball, build with blocks, hammer pegs, and finger-paint. All these playful activities develop and strengthen the skill necessary for handwriting.

Proper forming of letters requires complete relaxation of all the muscles not directly involved in the act of writing: the fingers and wrist should be relaxed, not tense. The forearm should pivot on the elbow to direct hand and pencil along the horizontal line of the paper.

To help students get ready to write, they should be taught to:

1. Sit up straight, leaning forward slightly
2. Rest both arms on the desk
3. Keep both feet on the floor
4. Relax

Handwriting will improve if practiced every day. Fifteen to twenty minutes a day is sufficient at this grade level. If the student is improving at a slower pace than is reasonable, chances are that the student needs more time doing readiness activities first. Don't be tempted to increase handwriting practice time–when readiness skills are developed enough, the student will improve in handwriting skills most efficiently without being pushed.

Left-Handedness

Make sure your students are using the hand that is most natural for them. If you are unsure, watch to see which hand your student uses to reach for things, which foot starts a flight of stairs, which hand he uses to throw a ball, and with which hand the student has the best fine motor skills (coloring, inserting a key, picking up a coin). The hand that predominates is the hand to be encouraged. Remember that left-handed students will have a more difficult task, because the movement from left to right across the page is awkward for the left hand.

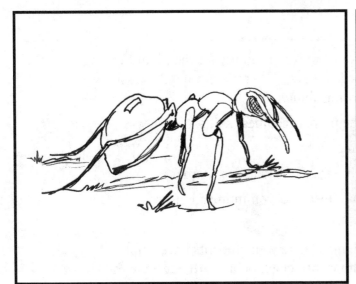 

ant   *bat*

Practice the small letter "a."

a   a

Practice the small letter "b."

b   b

Write a sentence using the word "ant."

Write a sentence using the word "bat."

Provide extra practice as needed on separate lined paper.

cat   *dog*

Practice the small letter "c."

c c

Practice the small letter "d."

d d

Write a sentence using the word "cat."

Write a sentence using the word "dog."

Provide extra practice as needed on separate lined paper.

eagle *fish*

Practice the small letter "e."

e *e*

Practice the small letter "f."

f *f*

Write a sentence using the word "eagle."

Write a sentence using the word "fish."

Provide extra practice as needed on separate lined paper.

goat   *hen*

Practice the small letter "g."

g g

Practice the small letter "h."

h h

Write a sentence using the word "goat."

Write a sentence using the word "hen."

Provide extra practice as needed on separate lined paper.

Addressing an Envelope

Copy the addressed envelope using the lines at the bottom of the page. Be sure to address the envelope in block form and place the return address correctly. Watch your slant and make each letter touch the baseline where it should. This exercise is for practice purposes. When addressing a real envelope, the postal service recommends that you write the addresses in manuscript form.

Jane Cooper
4800 Beach Avenue
Hammond, IN 46367

Mrs. Elizabeth Cooper
417 Illinois Avenue
Atlantic City, NJ 08401

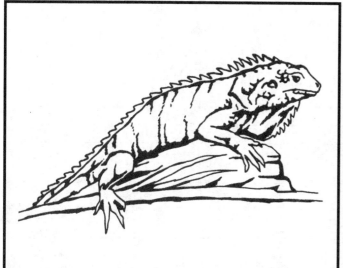

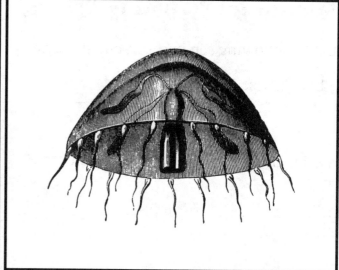

iguana

jellyfish

Practice the small letter "i."

i   i

Practice the small letter "j."

j   j

Write a sentence using the word "iguana."

Write a sentence using the word "jellyfish."

Provide extra practice as needed on separate lined paper.

Evaluate Your Writing Process

Copy the following sentences in cursive style.

The Lord loves a cheerful giver.

Blessed is the nation where God is the Lord.

Copy the following sentences in manuscript style.

Jesus Christ is the Son of God.

All true believers trust in Jesus Christ.

Answer the following questions.   Circle

		Yes	No
1.	Do all my letters slant in the same direction?	Yes	No
2.	Am I shaping every letter correctly?	Yes	No
3.	Are all my letters in one word connected?	Yes	No
4.	Am I spacing letters evenly?	Yes	No
5.	Am I leaving space between words?	Yes	No
6.	Am I including punctuation?	Yes	No
7.	Am I remembering to capitalize?	Yes	No

Letters I write well:

Letters I need to practice:

General Douglas MacArthur (1880-1964)

General Douglas MacArthur was a brave military leader who fought for the United States army during World War I, World War II, and the Korean War. MacArthur graduated with honors from the United States Military Academy at West Point a few years before the outbreak of World War I. This military hero and Christian gentleman often reminded the American people that in war there is no substitute for victory. As a young boy, MacArthur was schooled at home. Many of our country's great leaders learned in small one-room school houses. In your best penmanship, describe some of the blessings of learning at home.

kangaroo   *lamb*

Practice the small letter "k."

k *k*

Practice the small letter "l."

l *l*

Write a sentence using the word "kangaroo."

Write a sentence using the word "lamb."

Provide extra practice as needed on separate lined paper.

monkey   *newt*

Practice the small letter "m."

m m

Practice the small letter "n."

n n

Write a sentence using the word "monkey."

Write a sentence using the word "newt."

Provide extra practice as needed on separate lined paper.

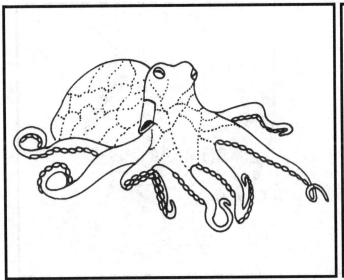 

octopus   *pony*

Practice the small letter "o."

o o

Practice the small letter "p."

p p

Write a sentence using the word "octopus."

Write a sentence using the word "pony."

Provide extra practice as needed on separate lined paper.

quail   *raccoon*

Practice the small letter "q."

q *q*

Practice the small letter "r."

r *r*

Write a sentence using the word "quail."

Write a sentence using the word "raccoon."

Provide extra practice as needed on separate lined paper.

shark   *tiger*

Practice the small letter "s."

s s

Practice the small letter "t."

t t

Write a sentence using the word "shark."

Write a sentence using the word "tiger."

Provide extra practice as needed on separate lined paper.

Writing a Short Letter

Write a letter to a friend. The main point of your letter should be to encourage a friend to read the Bible every day.

Your address _____

_____

Today's date _____

Dear _____ ,

_____

_____

_____

_____

_____

_____

_____

_____

Sincerely,

Your name _____

unicorn   *vulture*

Practice the small letter "u."

u u

Practice the small letter "v."

v v

Write a sentence using the word "unicorn."

Write a sentence using the word "vulture."

Provide extra practice as needed on separate lined paper.

Crossword Puzzle Exercise

Read Joshua 6:12-19 and work the crossword puzzle. Fill in the words in the right spaces on the puzzle as you read the story for today. "A" words go across; "D" words go down.

Joshua rose early in the morning, and the priests took up the **5-A** of the Lord. And **4-D** priests bore the seven trumpets of the **3-A** horns before the ark of the Lord. The armed **9-D** went before them. The second **2-D** they went around (compassed) the city once, and returned into the **6-D**: so they did **11-A** days. And on the seventh day it came to pass that after the seventh time they went around the city, the **10-A** blew with the trumpets, Joshua said to the people, "Shout; for the **1-A** hath given you the **6-A**." Joshua warned the people not to take anything out of the city of Jericho, for fear they would make the camp of Israel a **8-A**, and cause trouble. But all the silver and gold, and vessels of **7-D** and iron, being consecrated unto the Lord, were to go into the Lord's house.

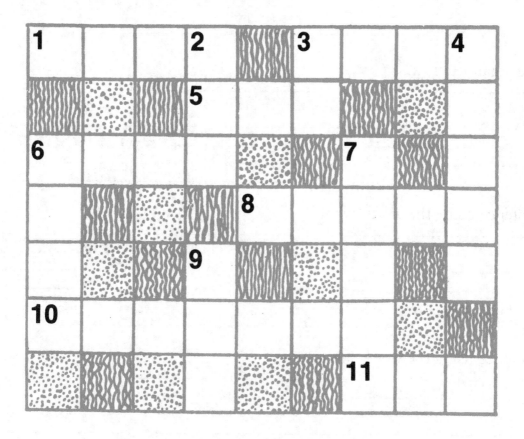

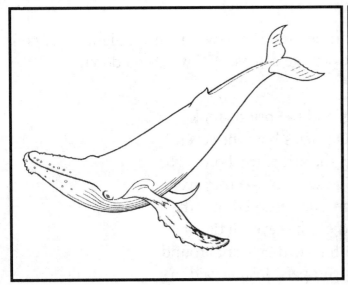

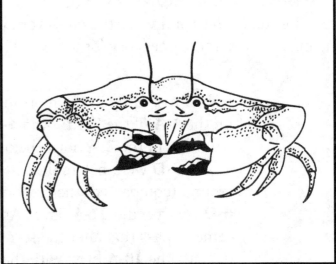

whale

xiphosuran
(i.e. crab)

Practice the small letter "w."

w w

Practice the small letter "x."

x x

Write a sentence using the word "whale."

Write a sentence using the word "xiphosuran."

Provide extra practice as needed on separate lined paper.

yak   *zebra*

Practice the small letter "y."

y y

Practice the small letter "z."

z z

Write a sentence using the word "yak."

Write a sentence using the word "zebra."

Provide extra practice as needed on separate lined paper.

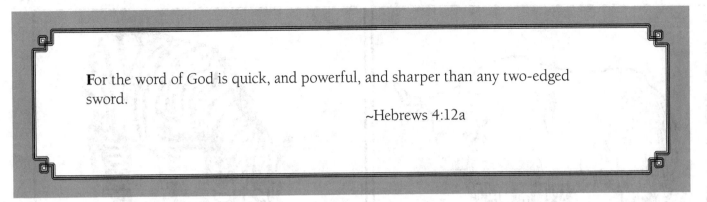

For the word of God is quick, and powerful, and sharper than any two-edged sword.

~Hebrews 4:12a

Instructor Tips

Help your students with difficult connecting strokes. Practice on extra paper before writing in the book is encouraged.

Chapter Check-up

Are you ready to write? Do your best work as you copy this sentence.
The world was created by the word of God.

Answer the following questions.   Circle

1.	Do all my letters slant in the same direction?	Yes	No
2.	Am I shaping every letter correctly?	Yes	No
3.	Are all the letters in one word connected?	Yes	No
4.	Am I spacing letters evenly?	Yes	No
5.	Am I leaving space between words?	Yes	No
6.	Am I leaving extra space between sentences?	Yes	No
7.	Am I remembering punctuation?	Yes	No
8.	Am I remembering to capitalize?	Yes	No

Letters I write well:

Letters I need to practice:

Abigail Adams (1744-1818)

Abigail received her primary education at home when she was young. In later years, Abigail married John Adams, who became America's second President. Abigail Adams became a devoted Christian mother who was well respected for her strong moral character and tender heart. In your best penmanship, write down two reasons why the United States needs to have godly mothers who will be faithful to their duties.

Write a Title for the Pictures

In your best cursive penmanship, give each picture a title. A good title is short, but tells enough to let someone know what is most interesting about the picture.

The first, second, fourth, and fifth pictures represent biblical places and people. Picture 1 is Bethlehem (Mt. 2:1-12, Lk. 2:1-20). Picture 2 is David (2 Samuel). Picture 4 is Jacob and Esau (Gen. 25:29-34). Picture 5 is Peter walking on the water (Mt. 14:22-33). If your students have not heard these Bible stories, they may have trouble with this exercise.

Solve the Clues

Write the word from this list that matches the meaning.

fun   idolatry   night   brave   foolish   nuts   Jesus

Squirrel Food   _____

God the Son   _____

Courageous   _____

Opposite of wise   _____

False worship   _____

Opposite of day   _____

Enjoyment   _____

Now write a sentence using at least three words from the word list at the top.

_____

_____

_____

Write a Headline

You are a newspaper editor! In your best printing, write a headline for each paragraph. A good headline is short but covers the most important facts of the story or paragraph.

_____

- -

_____

Our dog, Sarah, had puppies yesterday. There were four puppies. Two looked like her, and one looked like it's father. One was a mixture of Sarah and the other dog. Their names are Ruff, Peewee, Scarf, and Missy.

_____

- -

_____

Last week the Templetons went to the museum. They spent most of the time looking at the Indian exhibit, because Jaime and his sister, Lois, are interested in the Indian homes and costumes. One thing they saw was a Pawnee earth lodge. The Pawnees lived in Nebraska in houses made of earth. They moved to Oklahoma in 1876.

_____

- -

_____

Three things needed for fishing are bait, a hook, and some line. A pole makes fishing easier, but it is not needed. Worms are a good bait for many fish, but some fish like insects, minnows, or crayfish. It is very important to be quiet when fishing. Fish can hear in the water, and they will not bite if they are frightened.

_____

- -

_____

Benjamin Franklin was one of the men who helped organize the colonies into the United States. He accomplished many things. He wrote and printed a magazine called "Poor Richard's Almanac," he invented a more efficient stove for heating, and proved that lightning and electricity were different forms of the same thing. He was also an accomplished swimmer. He was not too shy to try anything that caught his interest.

_____

- -

_____

There were no horses in America when the first settlers arrived from Europe. All the horses in America are settlers from Europe, too. Most of the wild horses here came from horses that escaped from the Spanish explorers. Before the Europeans brought horses to America, the Plains Indians hunted buffalo on foot.

Practice Exercises

Practice writing the capital letters in cursive style.

Practice the capital letter "A."

a a

Practice the capital letter "B."

B B

Practice the capital letter "C."

C C

Practice the capital letter "D."

D D

Practice the capital letter "E."

E E

Practice the capital letter "F."

F F

Write the word "Battle" three times.

Practice Exercises

Practice writing the capital letters in cursive style.

Practice the capital letter "G."

Practice the capital letter "H."

Practice the capital letter "I."

Practice the capital letter "J."

Practice the capital letter "K."

Practice the capital letter "L."

Write the word "Jesus" three times.

Practice Exercises

Practice writing the capital letters in cursive style.

Practice the capital letter "M."

M M

Practice the capital letter "N."

N N

Practice the capital letter "O."

O O

Practice the capital letter "P."

P P

Practice the capital letter "Q."

Q Q

Practice the capital letter "R."

R R

Write the word "Rain" three times.

Practice Exercises

Practice writing the capital letters in cursive style.

Practice the capital letter "S."

Practice the capital letter "T."

Practice the capital letter "U."

Practice the capital letter "V."

Write the word "Savior" three times.

Write a sentence using the word "Savior."

Write a sentence using the word "Vacuum."

Practice Exercises

Practice writing the capital letters in cursive style.

Practice the capital letter "W."

$\mathcal{W}$ $\mathcal{W}$

Practice the capital letter "X."

$\mathcal{X}$ $\mathcal{X}$

Practice the capital letter "Y."

$\mathcal{Y}$ $\mathcal{Y}$

Practice the capital letter "Z."

$\mathcal{Z}$ $\mathcal{Z}$

Write the word "Yellow" three times.

Write a sentence using the word "Zebra."

Write a sentence using the word "Pennsylvania."

Writing a Business Letter

The greater number of marks of courtesy in a business letter make it different from a friendly letter. The *return address* and the *inside address* are the most obvious additions. A *colon* is used after the salutation rather than a comma. The *tone* is more formal, the *language* is more careful and reserved, and *formal titles* (Mr., Mrs., Dr.) are observed. Usually, business letters are typed, again as a courtesy.

Jerome Pavis
return address 555 Oak Street
Arlington, VT 00004
date March 29, 2003

Richard Mirling
Director, Customer Services
Edgebrook Toy Co.
55 E. Keystone Ave. inside address
Chicago, IL 60692

Mr. Mirling: salutation   body

I have enclosed a deluxe football I bought from a local store on January 28. The football has leak, and the store has gone out of business and cannot help me. I would like Edgebrook Toy Co. to repair or replace my football.

Thank you for your attention.

complimentary close Sincerely,
signature Jerome Pavis

Copy the letter for practice.

Writing a Business Letter

Write your own business letter to Leonard Mayson, President of General Cereals, 5555 Hialeah Road NW, Jacksonville, TX 75222, asking for information on the free digital watch his company offers. You need to know how many box tops to send and to what address they should be sent.

return address

date

inside address

salutation

body

complimentary close

signature

33

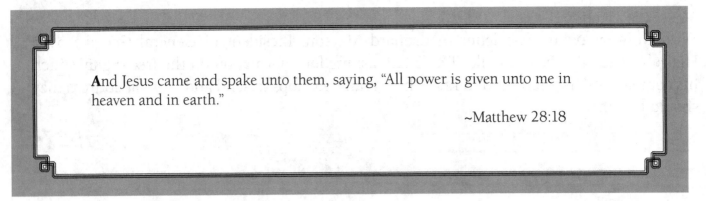

And Jesus came and spake unto them, saying, "All power is given unto me in heaven and in earth."

~Matthew 28:18

Instructor Tips

Help your students with difficult connecting strokes. Practice on extra paper is encouraged.

Chapter Check-up

Are you ready to write? Do your best work as you copy this sentence.
God gives power and grace to His people.

Answer the following questions.   Circle

1.	Do all my letters slant in the same direction?	Yes	No
2.	Am I shaping every letter correctly?	Yes	No
3.	Are all the letters in one word connected?	Yes	No
4.	Am I spacing letters evenly?	Yes	No
5.	Am I leaving space between words?	Yes	No
6.	Am I leaving extra space between sentences?	Yes	No
7.	Am I remembering punctuation?	Yes	No
8.	Am I remembering to capitalize?	Yes	No

Letters I write well:

Letters I need to practice:

Theodore Roosevelt (1858-1919)

Did you know that Theodore Roosevelt was taught at home by his mother? Theodore learned at an early age to make good use of his time. This Christian gentleman became President of the United States at the age of 43. During his time as President, Roosevelt began to set up a system of national parks and also developed other programs to protect our national resources. President Roosevelt wanted to help preserve the God-given beauty of our nation's forests and streams. In your best penmanship, write down three things that you can do to help keep America beautiful.

Crossword Puzzle Exercise

Read in Genesis 3:9-12 how Adam tried to excuse himself for his sin. Then do the puzzle. "A" words go across; "D" words go down.

The Lord **1-D** called unto **6-D** and said, "Where **7-A** thou?"

Adam said, "I heard thy **3-A** in the **5-D**, and I was **9-A**, because I was naked; and I hid myself."

God said, "Have you eaten of the fruit of the **8-D** that I **4-D** you not to eat?"

And the **2-A** said, "The woman gave **2-D** fruit from the tree, and I did eat."

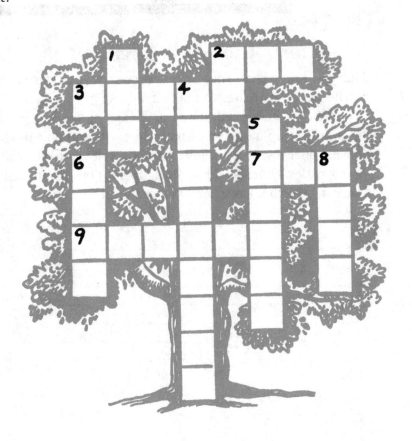

Creating Words

See how many words you can make using the letters in the words below. Use each letter only once as you make new words. One word, for example, is *nation*. Try to make at least ten new words.

generation

_____

_____

_____

_____

_____

_____

_____

_____

_____

_____

constitutional

_____

_____

_____

_____

_____

_____

_____

_____

_____

_____

_____

Creating Words

See how many words you can make using the letters in the words below. Use each letter only once as you make new words. One word, for example, is *pop*. Try to make at least ten new words.

porcupine

radiological

Number Exercises on the Calendar

Write the missing numbers into the calendar below.

September

Sun.	Mon.	Tue.	Wed.	Thu.	Fri.	Sat.
					1	2
3					8	
			13			
17						23
					29	

Connecting Letters

Trace and practice the connecting exercises listed below. These exercises will help you to connect letters with greater accuracy.

abc

def

ghi

jkl

mno

pqr

stuv

wxyz

Spacing Exercise

Write the correct word in each space.

"In the _____ God _____

the _____ and the _____."

Genesis 1:1

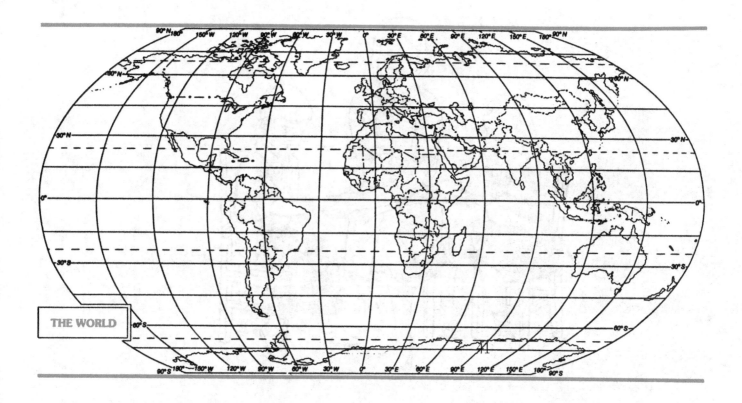

THE WORLD

"Praise ye the _____. O _____ thanks

_____ the _____; for he _____ _____:

for his _____ endureth _____ _____."

Psalm 106:1

41

Spacing Exercise

Write the correct word in each space.

"Remember _____ thy _____ in _____ days of ___ _____, while the _____ days come not, ___ _____ years draw _____, when _____ shalt _____, I have _____ _____ in _____;" Ecclesiastes 12:1

"Be ye _____ _____ of ____, as dear _____: And walk ___ _____, as Christ _____ hath _____ ___, and hath _____ _____ for ___ an _____ and a sacrifice _____ for a sweet smelling _____." Ephesians 5:1-2

42

Abbreviations: Days of the Week

An abbreviation is a short way to write a word. Periods are used after the abbreviation. Making a calendar is a good exercise for this page.

Sun.   Mon.   Tue.   Wed.   Thu.   Fri.   Sat.

Practice the abbreviations given above for the days of the week. Copy each abbreviation five times.

Abbreviations: Months of the Year

Note that the months May, June, and July are not abbreviated because they are already short words. Making a calendar is a good exercise for this page.

Jan.   **Feb.**   **Mar.**   **Apr.**   **May**   **June**

July   **Aug.**   **Sept.**   **Oct.**   **Nov.**   **Dec.**

Practice the abbreviations given above for the months of the year. Copy each abbreviation three times.

Word Store

Write your own letter using all the words from the "word store."

Gift   Bible   Friend   Thursday   Party

return address

date

salutation

body

complimentary close

signature

Alphabetizing

In the dictionary and in the telephone directory, words are listed in alphabetical order. Words that begin with "a" come first, then words that begin with "b," and so on. These words are in alphabetical order.

ax   boy   car   dog   eat   fry   go   home   ice   jar

Write these words in alphabetical order.

bone   door   ask   cat

_____

- -

_____

pan   nation   open   mail   quite

_____

- -

_____

The following groups are a little more difficult. Some of the letters in the alphabet are skipped. Write these words in alphabetical order.

bone   eagle   cart   go

_____

- -

_____

pan   eagle   open   cart   bone

_____

- -

_____

telephone   man   woman   house

_____

- -

_____

zoo   apple   open   fill   spin

_____

- -

_____

north   zebra   kind   ant   monkey   giraffe

_____

- -

_____

Alphabetizing

How do we alphabetize words that begin with the same letter? We have to look at the second letter, and put those into alphabetical order just like in the dictionary. These words are in alphabetical order.

able   acre   add   after   age   ahead   air   ajar

See if you can put the following words in alphabetical order.

break   bean   bicycle   blue

_____

_____

mat   mine   mutt   moon   meat

_____

_____

nod   neat   nut   nail   nice

_____

_____

old   over   oat   on   open

_____

_____

Sometimes the first and second letters are both used to put words in alphabetical order.

able   **ac**re   **ba**ll   **be**ll   **ca**ll   **cr**ew   **cu**t

act   bug   and   band

_____

_____

dune   cat   but   dot   bat   cup

_____

_____

Here's a really hard one. Ready?
boil   meal   bill   made   bat   acre   bend   older   eat

_____

_____

_____

_____

Susanna Wesley

Susanna Wesley received her primary education at home. She grew up to be a loving Christian mother of nineteen children. Two of Mrs. Wesley's children, John and Charles, became famous Christian ministers and hymn writers. Read Proverbs 31:10-31. In your best penmanship, write down three things that a godly mother will do for her family.

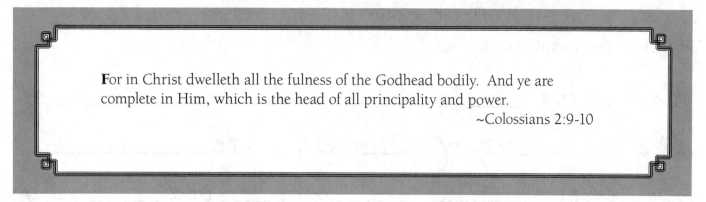

For in Christ dwelleth all the fulness of the Godhead bodily. And ye are complete in Him, which is the head of all principality and power.

~Colossians 2:9-10

Instructor Tips

Help your students with difficult connecting strokes. Practice on extra paper should be encouraged.

Chapter Check-up

Are you ready to write? Do your best work as you copy this sentence.
Jesus Christ is King of Kings and very God.

Answer the following questions.   Circle

1.	Do all my letters slant in the same direction?	Yes	No
2.	Am I shaping every letter correctly?	Yes	No
3.	Are all the letters in one word connected?	Yes	No
4.	Am I spacing letters evenly?	Yes	No
5.	Am I leaving space between words?	Yes	No
6.	Am I leaving extra space between sentences?	Yes	No
7.	Am I remembering punctuation?	Yes	No
8.	Am I remembering to capitalize?	Yes	No

Letters I write well:

Letters I need to practice:

Spacing Exercise

Write the correct word in each space.

"Knowing _____ _____, that no _____ of the _____ is of _____ private _____. For the _____ _____ not _____ old _____ by the _____ of _____: but _____ men _____ _____ spake as _____ were _____ by the _____ _____." 2 Peter 1:20-21

"For _____ is _____ of _____, that _____ _____ his _____: and _____ commandments are _____ _____." 1 John 5:3

Writing Exercise

Complete the paragraph with your own words in cursive style.

I love to study the Bible because

Old Testament Books

Starting with Genesis, write the thirty-nine books of the Old Testament in cursive style.

Genesis

New Testament Books

Starting with Matthew, write the twenty-seven books of the New Testament in cursive style.

Matthew,

Oceans and Continents

Write the names of the oceans and continents in the spaces below.

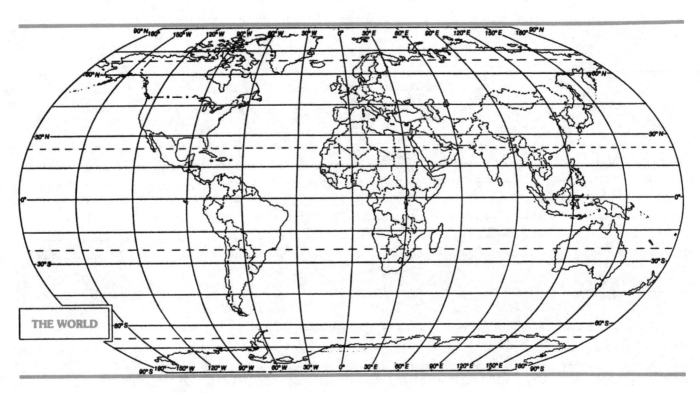

THE WORLD

Oceans

_____

_____

_____

_____

_____

_____

_____

_____

_____

_____

_____

Continents

_____

_____

_____

_____

_____

_____

_____

_____

_____

_____

_____

Writing Exercise

Complete the paragraph with your own words in cursive style.

I need to pray for my family because

Writing Exercise
Copy the following sentence three times.

True Christian liberty is not the right to live as we please, but the power to live as God requires.

Writing Exercise
Copy the following Bible verse three times.

"Where there is no vision, the people perish;
but he who keeps the Law, blessed is he."
~Proverbs 29:18

Writing Exercise

Complete the paragraph with your own words in cursive style.

I think learning at home has helped me because

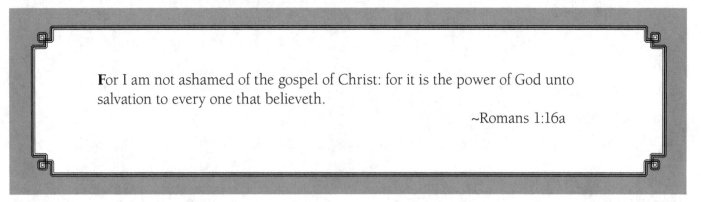

For I am not ashamed of the gospel of Christ: for it is the power of God unto salvation to every one that believeth.

~Romans 1:16a

Instructor Tips

Help your students with difficult connecting strokes. Practice on extra paper should be encouraged.

Chapter Check-up

Are you ready to write? Do your best work as you copy this sentence.
The Bible says to do all things decently and in order.

Answer the following questions.   Circle

1. Do all my letters slant in the same direction?	Yes	No
2. Am I shaping every letter correctly?	Yes	No
3. Are all the letters in one word connected?	Yes	No
4. Am I spacing letters evenly?	Yes	No
5. Am I leaving space between words?	Yes	No
6. Am I leaving extra space between sentences?	Yes	No
7. Am I remembering punctuation?	Yes	No
8. Am I remembering to capitalize?	Yes	No

Letters I write well:

Letters I need to practice: